POP ART MAKEUP

© 2024 QuillScribe Memoirs

INTRODUCTION

PREPARATION:

START WITH A CLEAN, MOISTURIZED FACE. GATHER CLEAN TOOLS AND FACE PAINTS.

BASE APPLICATION:

APPLY THE BASE COLOR EVENLY WITH A SPONGE. ENSURE A SMOOTH AND EVEN LAYER.

DETAILING:

USE FINE BRUSHES FOR INTRICATE DESIGNS. BEGIN WITH LARGER ELEMENTS AND FINISH WITH SMALL DETAILS.

LAYERING:

LET EACH LAYER DRY BEFORE ADDING ANOTHER. SET WITH TRANSLUCENT POWDER IF NEEDED.

FINAL TOUCHES:

ADD HIGHLIGHTS OR GLITTER. USE SETTING SPRAY TO LOCK IN THE DESIGN.

CLEAN-UP:

REMOVE MAKEUP WITH GENTLE REMOVER, WASH FACE, AND MOISTURIZE.

SAFETY GUIDELINES

SAFE PRODUCTS:

USE ONLY SKIN-SAFE, COSMETIC-GRADE FACE PAINTS.

PATCH TEST:

TEST PRODUCTS ON A SMALL AREA OF SKIN FOR ALLERGIES BEFORE FULL APPLICATION.

HYGIENE:

SANITIZE HANDS AND TOOLS. DON'T APPLY ON BROKEN OR IRRITATED SKIN.

SENSITIVE AREAS:

BE CAREFUL AROUND EYES AND MOUTH. USE APPROPRIATE PRODUCTS FOR THESE AREAS.

SUPERVISION:

KEEP CHILDREN SUPERVISED DURING APPLICATION.

GENTLE REMOVAL:

REMOVE PAINT CAREFULLY WITH MAKEUP REMOVER AND AVOID HARSH SCRUBBING.

BY FOLLOWING THESE INSTRUCTIONS AND GUIDELINES, YOU CAN CREATE SAFE AND BEAUTIFUL FACE PAINT DESIGNS.

MYSTIC MERMAID

BASE COLOR:

APPLY A LIGHT FOUNDATION TO EVEN OUT THE SKIN TONE AND CREATE A SMOOTH CANVAS.

EYE MAKEUP:

USE A FLAT BRUSH TO APPLY VIBRANT PURPLE EYESHADOW AROUND THE EYES, EXTENDING IT OUTWARD TO CREATE A DRAMATIC WING.

ADD A TOUCH OF BLUE EYESHADOW NEAR THE INNER CORNERS OF THE EYES FOR A GRADIENT EFFECT.

FINISH THE EYES WITH BLACK EYELINER AND FALSE LASHES FOR A BOLD LOOK.

SCALES DESIGN:

USING A STENCIL OR FREEHAND WITH A DETAIL BRUSH, PAINT TEAL AND BLUE SCALES EXTENDING FROM THE FOREHEAD DOWN TO THE CHEEKS.

ADD HIGHLIGHTS WITH A LIGHTER COLOR TO GIVE THE SCALES A THREE-DIMENSIONAL, SHIMMERING EFFECT.

LIPS:

APPLY DEEP PURPLE LIPSTICK WITH A LIP BRUSH, ENSURING A CLEAN AND VIBRANT FINISH.

HAIR AND NECK:

IF DESIRED, PAINT THE HAIRLINE WITH TEAL AND BLUE FACE PAINT TO BLEND WITH THE SCALES. USE A TEMPORARY HAIR COLOR SPRAY TO ADD SIMILAR HUES TO YOUR HAIR.

PAINT MATCHING SCALES ON THE NECK AND COLLARBONE AREA FOR A COHESIVE LOOK.

FINAL TOUCHES:

ENSURE ALL ELEMENTS ARE SYMMETRICAL AND VIBRANT. USE SETTING SPRAY TO KEEP THE MAKEUP INTACT. ADD SOME SHIMMER OR GLITTER TO ENHANCE THE AQUATIC THEME.

GALACTIC GUARDIAN

BASE MASK:

START BY APPLYING A TURQUOISE BASE TO THE UPPER FACE USING A MAKEUP SPONGE, COVERING THE FOREHEAD, AROUND THE EYES, AND DOWN TO THE UPPER CHEEKS.

PURPLE AND BLACK DETAILS:

USE A FLAT BRUSH TO APPLY PURPLE FACE PAINT ON THE OUTER EDGES OF THE TURQUOISE MASK, BLENDING INWARD TO CREATE DEPTH.

OUTLINE THE MASK WITH BLACK FACE PAINT USING A FINE BRUSH, CREATING SHARP AND CLEAN LINES TO DEFINE THE EDGES AND DETAILS.

GREEN GEM DESIGN:

PAINT A GREEN CIRCLE IN THE CENTER OF THE FOREHEAD WITH A DETAIL BRUSH, REPRESENTING A FUTURISTIC GEM. ADD HIGHLIGHTS WITH A LIGHTER GREEN TO GIVE IT A 3D EFFECT.

EYE MAKEUP:

APPLY VIBRANT PURPLE EYESHADOW AROUND THE EYES, BLENDING INTO THE MASK. USE BLACK EYELINER FOR A BOLD, WINGED EFFECT, AND FINISH WITH FALSE LASHES.

LIPS:

APPLY METALLIC PURPLE LIPSTICK USING A LIP BRUSH FOR A BOLD, FUTURISTIC LOOK.

FINAL TOUCHES:

ENSURE ALL ELEMENTS ARE BALANCED AND SHARP. USE SETTING SPRAY TO SECURE THE MAKEUP, AND ADD ANY ADDITIONAL HIGHLIGHTS OR DETAILS TO ENHANCE THE FUTURISTIC THEME.

MYSTIC SKULL

BASE COLOR:

APPLY WHITE FACE PAINT EVENLY ACROSS THE ENTIRE FACE USING A MAKEUP SPONGE, CREATING A SMOOTH BASE.

MASK DESIGN:

WITH A FLAT BRUSH, APPLY BLUE FACE PAINT IN A MASK SHAPE AROUND THE EYES, COVERING THE FOREHEAD AND TEMPLES.

OUTLINE THE MASK WITH BLACK PAINT USING A FINE BRUSH, ADDING SHARP, CLEAN LINES FOR DEFINITION.

FOREHEAD AND CHEEK DETAILS:

PAINT A YELLOW DIAMOND SHAPE IN THE CENTER OF THE FOREHEAD WITH A DETAIL BRUSH, BORDERED BY BLUE AND BLACK FOR A 3D EFFECT.

ADD BLACK TRIANGULAR SHAPES ON THE CHEEKS AND SMALL DOTS AROUND THE MASK FOR ADDITIONAL DETAIL.

EYE MAKEUP:

APPLY PURPLE EYESHADOW AROUND THE EYES, BLENDING INTO THE BLUE MASK. USE BLACK EYELINER FOR A BOLD LOOK, AND FINISH WITH FALSE LASHES.

MOUTH AND NOSE:

PAINT A BLACK TRIANGLE ON THE TIP OF THE NOSE USING A DETAIL BRUSH.

CREATE A STITCHED MOUTH EFFECT BY DRAWING BLACK LINES FROM THE CORNERS OF THE MOUTH ACROSS THE CHEEKS, WITH SMALL VERTICAL LINES INTERSECTING THEM.

FINAL TOUCHES:

DOUBLE-CHECK FOR SYMMETRY AND ADD ANY NECESSARY TOUCH-UPS. USE SETTING SPRAY TO KEEP THE MAKEUP IN PLACE.

BROKEN DOLL

BASE COLOR:

APPLY A BRIGHT BLUE FACE PAINT EVENLY ACROSS THE ENTIRE FACE USING A MAKEUP SPONGE, COVERING FROM THE FOREHEAD TO THE CHIN.

MASK AND EYE DESIGN:

WITH A FLAT BRUSH, PAINT A BLACK AND WHITE CRACKED MASK PATTERN AROUND THE EYES AND ACROSS THE FACE, GIVING IT A FRAGMENTED LOOK.

APPLY PURPLE EYESHADOW AROUND THE EYES, BLENDING IT INTO THE BLACK OF THE MASK. USE BLACK EYELINER TO DEFINE THE EYES, CREATING A SHARP, INTENSE LOOK.

FOREHEAD AND CHEEK DETAILS:

ADD BLACK CRACKS AND LINES ACROSS THE FOREHEAD AND CHEEKS USING A FINE BRUSH, EMPHASIZING THE CRACKED MASK EFFECT.

PLACE A SMALL RED DOT ON THE FOREHEAD FOR AN ADDITIONAL FOCAL POINT.

MOUTH AND NOSE:

PAINT A BLACK TRIANGLE ON THE TIP OF THE NOSE WITH A DETAIL BRUSH.

CREATE A STITCHED MOUTH EFFECT WITH BLACK LINES EXTENDING FROM THE CORNERS OF THE MOUTH, INTERSECTED BY VERTICAL LINES.

LIPS:

APPLY A BOLD RED LIPSTICK WITH A LIP BRUSH, ENSURING THE LIPS ARE SHARPLY DEFINED.

FINAL TOUCHES:

CHECK THE SYMMETRY OF THE DESIGN AND MAKE ANY NECESSARY ADJUSTMENTS. USE SETTING SPRAY TO KEEP THE MAKEUP INTACT THROUGHOUT THE EVENT.

Zombie Siren

Base Color:

Apply a vibrant green face paint evenly over the entire face and neck using a makeup sponge to create a smooth, even base.

Eye Design:

Use a flat brush to apply a deep blue or teal eyeshadow around the eyes, extending outwards for a dramatic effect.

Add black eyeliner to define the eyes, with a winged shape extending toward the temples. Finish with false lashes for intensity.

Wound Effects:

With a detail brush, paint black and red jagged wound-like shapes on the forehead, cheeks, and neck to simulate torn skin.

Add shading around the wounds with dark red and black to create depth and a more realistic look.

Lips:

Apply a bold red lipstick using a lip brush, ensuring the edges are sharp and clean. Add a bit of black shading on one side for a more dramatic effect.

Details and Highlights:

Add small, yellowish-green dots within some of the wound areas using a fine brush to give a more infected, eerie appearance.

Use a lighter green or yellow face paint to highlight certain areas of the face, like the forehead and cheekbones, to give dimension.

Final Touches:

Make sure all designs are balanced and the wounds look three-dimensional. Use setting spray to keep the makeup in place throughout your event.

NIGHTMARE BAT

BASE COLOR:

APPLY A BRIGHT BLUE FACE PAINT EVENLY OVER THE ENTIRE FACE AND NECK USING A MAKEUP SPONGE TO CREATE A SMOOTH, VIBRANT BASE.

EYE DESIGN:

USE A FLAT BRUSH TO PAINT ONE EYE AREA WITH RED FACE PAINT AND THE OTHER WITH PURPLE, EXTENDING THE COLORS OUTWARDS WITH JAGGED, DRIPPING EDGES.

ADD BLACK EYELINER AROUND BOTH EYES, EXTENDING INTO A DRAMATIC WING FOR A SHARP, INTENSE LOOK. FINISH WITH FALSE LASHES.

FOREHEAD BAT DESIGN:

WITH A FINE BRUSH, PAINT A BLACK BAT SHAPE IN THE CENTER OF THE FOREHEAD. MAKE SURE THE BAT'S WINGS EXTEND ACROSS THE BROW LINE, WITH SHARP, DEFINED EDGES.

LIPS:

APPLY RED LIPSTICK USING A LIP BRUSH, ENSURING A CLEAN AND BOLD FINISH. ADD A SMALL AMOUNT OF BLACK FACE PAINT TO THE CORNERS FOR A SUBTLE OMBRE EFFECT.

DETAILS AND SHADING:

USE BLACK FACE PAINT TO ADD CRACKS AND SMALL DETAILS AROUND THE EYES, NOSE, AND MOUTH, GIVING A CRACKED OR FRACTURED APPEARANCE.

HIGHLIGHT CERTAIN AREAS WITH A LIGHTER BLUE OR WHITE PAINT, ESPECIALLY AROUND THE BAT DESIGN AND CHEEKBONES, TO ADD DEPTH.

FINAL TOUCHES:

DOUBLE-CHECK FOR SYMMETRY AND ENSURE ALL DESIGNS ARE SHARP AND VIVID. USE A SETTING SPRAY TO LOCK THE MAKEUP IN PLACE FOR LONG-LASTING WEAR.

Gory Glam Zombie

Base Color:

Apply a vibrant green face paint evenly over the entire face and neck using a makeup sponge to create a smooth, even base.

Eye Design:

Use a fine brush to apply black face paint around the eyes, extending it outwards with jagged, sharp edges. Add some red eyeshadow around the eyes for added depth.

Use black eyeliner to define the eyes, extending the line into a dramatic wing, and finish with false lashes for a bold look.

Forehead and Nose Details:

Paint a dripping red circle in the center of the forehead with a flat brush, adding black cracks around it for a shattered effect.

Create a small, dripping wound on the nose using red face paint, blending with black for depth.

Mouth and Cheek Wounds:

Use a fine brush to paint a large, torn wound on one cheek, using black and red face paint to create depth. Add small yellow dots inside to mimic teeth or infection.

Apply red lipstick to the lips, blending slightly with black paint on the corners for a distressed look. Add dripping red paint below the lips to simulate blood.

Neck and Additional Details:

Extend the design onto the neck, painting more dripping blood effects and small wounds. Use black and red face paint to create a cohesive look with the face.

Highlight certain areas with a lighter green or yellow paint to add dimension, especially around the wounds and cheekbones.

Final Touches:

Ensure all designs are sharp and symmetrical, with wounds looking realistic and three-dimensional. Use a setting spray to keep the makeup intact throughout the event.

HAUNTED BEAUTY

BASE COLOR:

USE A MAKEUP SPONGE TO EVENLY APPLY A GREENISH-BLUE FACE PAINT ACROSS THE ENTIRE FACE.

EYE MAKEUP:

PAINT A PURPLE MASK AROUND THE EYES USING A FLAT BRUSH.

OUTLINE THE MASK WITH A FINE BRUSH IN BLACK, ADDING CRACKS FOR DETAIL.

FINISH THE EYES WITH BLACK EYELINER AND FALSE EYELASHES.

ADDITIONAL EYES:

WITH A DETAIL BRUSH, PAINT SMALL GREEN EYE-LIKE DESIGNS ON ONE SIDE OF THE MASK.

LIPS:

APPLY A DEEP RED LIPSTICK WITH A LIP BRUSH, THEN OUTLINE THE LIPS WITH BLACK FOR CONTRAST.

COLLAR AND NECK:

PAINT A CHOKER AROUND THE NECK USING A FLAT BRUSH, ADDING RED DOTS WITH A DETAIL BRUSH.

BLOOD EFFECT:

CREATE DRIPPING BLOOD EFFECTS USING A SMALL SPONGE OR FINE BRUSH WITH RED PAINT AROUND THE MASK AND COLLAR.

MONOCHROME ELEGANCE

BASE COLOR:

START WITH A NATURAL SKIN TONE AS THE BASE, APPLYING A LIGHT FOUNDATION TO CREATE A SMOOTH AND FLAWLESS COMPLEXION.

EYE DESIGN:

USE BLACK FACE PAINT TO CREATE A BOLD, SPIKY DESIGN EXTENDING FROM THE EYES OUTWARD. MAKE SURE THE SPIKES ARE SHARP AND SYMMETRICAL ON BOTH SIDES.

APPLY BLACK EYESHADOW TO THE EYELIDS, BLENDING IT INTO THE SPIKY DESIGN. ADD WHITE EYELINER OR EYESHADOW TO THE LOWER LASH LINE TO CREATE CONTRAST.

EYEBROWS:

DARKEN AND SHAPE THE EYEBROWS WITH BLACK FACE PAINT OR AN EYEBROW PENCIL, CREATING A SHARP, DEFINED ARCH.

LIPS:

APPLY BLACK LIPSTICK USING A LIP BRUSH, ENSURING A CLEAN AND BOLD FINISH THAT COMPLEMENTS THE EYE DESIGN.

FOREHEAD DETAIL:

USE A FINE BRUSH TO PAINT A SLEEK, CURVED BLACK LINE EXTENDING FROM THE FOREHEAD DOWN TOWARDS ONE EYE, ADDING AN ELEGANT TOUCH TO THE DESIGN.

FINAL TOUCHES:

ENSURE ALL LINES AND SHAPES ARE SHARP AND PRECISE. USE SETTING SPRAY TO KEEP THE MAKEUP INTACT AND LONG-LASTING.

DEADLY NURSE

BASE COLOR:

APPLY A LIGHT FOUNDATION OVER THE ENTIRE FACE TO CREATE A SMOOTH AND EVEN BASE.

EYE MAKEUP:

USE A FLAT BRUSH TO APPLY RED EYESHADOW AROUND THE EYES, BLENDING IT OUTWARD FOR A DRAMATIC EFFECT.

DEFINE THE EYES WITH BLACK EYELINER, CREATING A SHARP WING. ADD BLACK SPIKY DESIGNS EXTENDING FROM THE LOWER LASH LINE TO MIMIC DRIPPING EFFECTS.

FINISH THE EYE LOOK WITH FALSE LASHES FOR ADDED INTENSITY.

FOREHEAD DESIGN:

PAINT A RED CROSS IN THE CENTER OF THE FOREHEAD USING A FINE BRUSH. ADD A SMALL DROP EFFECT AT THE BOTTOM OF THE CROSS FOR A MORE DRAMATIC LOOK.

CHEEK BLOOD EFFECT:

USE A FINE BRUSH TO ADD BLACK DRIPPING EFFECTS BENEATH THE EYES, BLENDING THEM INTO THE RED EYESHADOW FOR A COHESIVE LOOK.

LIPS:

APPLY A VIBRANT RED LIPSTICK USING A LIP BRUSH, ENSURING THE EDGES ARE CLEAN AND BOLD.

FINAL TOUCHES:

ENSURE ALL DESIGNS ARE SHARP AND SYMMETRICAL. USE A SETTING SPRAY TO KEEP THE MAKEUP INTACT FOR LONG-LASTING WEAR.

BLOODTHIRSTY NURSE

BASE COLOR:

START WITH YOUR NATURAL SKIN TONE, APPLYING A LIGHT FOUNDATION TO CREATE A FLAWLESS, EVEN BASE.

EYE MAKEUP:

USE A FLAT BRUSH TO APPLY BOLD RED EYESHADOW AROUND THE EYES, BLENDING IT OUTWARD AND UPWARD TOWARDS THE TEMPLES.

APPLY BLACK EYELINER TO DEFINE THE EYES, CREATING A DRAMATIC WINGED EFFECT. ADD FALSE LASHES FOR A MORE INTENSE LOOK.

FOREHEAD DESIGN:

WITH A FINE BRUSH, PAINT A RED CROSS ON THE FOREHEAD, EXTENDING DOWN TOWARDS THE EYEBROWS. ENSURE THE LINES ARE SHARP AND SYMMETRICAL.

CHEEK BLOOD EFFECT:

USE A FINE BRUSH TO PAINT A DRIPPING BLOOD EFFECT ON ONE CHEEK, STARTING WITH A SOLID RED SHAPE AND BLENDING IT DOWNWARD INTO THIN, DRIPPING LINES FOR A REALISTIC APPEARANCE.

LIPS:

APPLY A DEEP RED LIPSTICK WITH A LIP BRUSH, ENSURING A CLEAN AND BOLD FINISH THAT MATCHES THE INTENSITY OF THE EYES AND CHEEK DESIGN.

FINAL TOUCHES:

DOUBLE-CHECK THAT ALL DESIGNS ARE SHARP, AND THE BLOOD EFFECTS ARE REALISTIC. USE A SETTING SPRAY TO KEEP THE MAKEUP IN PLACE THROUGHOUT THE EVENT.

BUTTERFLY ENCHANTRESS

BASE COLOR:

START WITH A NATURAL SKIN TONE FOUNDATION, APPLYING IT EVENLY TO CREATE A FLAWLESS BASE FOR THE INTRICATE DESIGNS.

BUTTERFLY WING DESIGN:

USE A FINE BRUSH TO PAINT BUTTERFLY WING SHAPES EXTENDING FROM THE FOREHEAD DOWN TO THE CHEEKS. BEGIN WITH LIGHT BLUE ON THE UPPER PARTS OF THE WINGS AND BLEND INTO DARKER BLUE AND BLACK NEAR THE EDGES.

ADD DETAILS TO THE WINGS WITH BLACK FACE PAINT, CREATING SYMMETRICAL LINES AND DOTS TO MIMIC THE TEXTURE OF REAL BUTTERFLY WINGS. INCORPORATE WHITE DOTS ALONG THE BLACK EDGES FOR ADDED REALISM.

EYE MAKEUP:

APPLY PURPLE EYESHADOW AROUND THE EYES, BLENDING IT OUTWARD INTO THE WING DESIGN. USE BLACK EYELINER TO CREATE A SHARP WINGED EFFECT, EXTENDING IT INTO THE BUTTERFLY WINGS.

ADD FALSE LASHES TO ENHANCE THE EYES, MAKING THEM LOOK LARGER AND MORE DRAMATIC.

LIPS:

APPLY A BOLD PURPLE LIPSTICK USING A LIP BRUSH, ENSURING THE COLOR IS VIBRANT AND MATCHES THE PURPLE IN THE EYE MAKEUP.

FOREHEAD AND CHEEK DETAILS:

PAINT ADDITIONAL DECORATIVE ELEMENTS ON THE FOREHEAD, SUCH AS SMALL, BLACK ORNAMENTAL SHAPES THAT BLEND INTO THE BUTTERFLY WINGS.

ADD SUBTLE SWIRLS OR LINES ON THE CHEEKS TO TIE THE LOOK TOGETHER, ENHANCING THE OVERALL BUTTERFLY THEME.

FINAL TOUCHES:

DOUBLE-CHECK THAT ALL DESIGNS ARE SYMMETRICAL AND THE COLORS ARE WELL BLENDED. USE SETTING SPRAY TO SECURE THE MAKEUP FOR LONG-LASTING WEAR.

CONSIDER ADDING BUTTERFLY-THEMED ACCESSORIES, SUCH AS EARRINGS OR A HAIRPIECE, TO COMPLEMENT THE FACE PAINT.

ENCHANTED SORCERESS

BASE COLOR:

APPLY A SMOOTH LAYER OF GREEN FACE PAINT OVER THE ENTIRE FACE AND NECK USING A MAKEUP SPONGE TO CREATE AN EVEN BASE.

EYE MAKEUP:

USE A FLAT BRUSH TO APPLY PURPLE EYESHADOW AROUND THE EYES, BLENDING IT OUTWARD FOR A DRAMATIC EFFECT.

DEFINE THE EYES WITH BLACK EYELINER, EXTENDING IT INTO A WINGED SHAPE. ADD BLACK DOTS BELOW THE EYES FOR A STRIKING, DETAILED EFFECT.

FINISH WITH FALSE LASHES TO ENHANCE THE EYES AND GIVE THEM A MORE DRAMATIC APPEARANCE.

EYEBROWS:

SHAPE AND DARKEN THE EYEBROWS USING A BLACK EYEBROW PENCIL OR FACE PAINT, CREATING A SHARP, DEFINED ARCH THAT COMPLEMENTS THE EYE DESIGN.

LIPS:

APPLY A BOLD PURPLE LIPSTICK USING A LIP BRUSH, ENSURING THE COLOR IS VIBRANT AND MATCHES THE PURPLE IN THE EYE MAKEUP.

CONTOUR AND HIGHLIGHTS:

LIGHTLY CONTOUR THE CHEEKBONES WITH A DARKER GREEN SHADE TO ADD DEPTH AND DEFINITION. HIGHLIGHT THE CENTER OF THE FOREHEAD, NOSE, AND CHIN WITH A LIGHTER GREEN OR YELLOW TO ENHANCE THE DIMENSIONALITY OF THE FACE.

FINAL TOUCHES:

DOUBLE-CHECK FOR SYMMETRY AND ENSURE ALL LINES AND COLORS ARE SHARP AND WELL BLENDED. USE SETTING SPRAY TO SECURE THE MAKEUP FOR LONG-LASTING WEAR.

ADD COMPLEMENTARY ACCESSORIES LIKE HORNS OR JEWELRY TO COMPLETE THE LOOK.

CARNIVAL DREAM

BASE COLOR:

START WITH A NATURAL SKIN TONE FOUNDATION, APPLYING IT EVENLY TO CREATE A SMOOTH, FLAWLESS BASE.

EYE MAKEUP:

USE A FLAT BRUSH TO APPLY VIBRANT PURPLE EYESHADOW AROUND THE EYES, BLENDING IT OUTWARD TOWARD THE TEMPLES.

WITH A SMALLER BRUSH, ADD A TURQUOISE BAND OF COLOR BELOW THE EYES, EXTENDING IT OUTWARD. ADD SMALL, COLORFUL DOTS IN VARIOUS SHADES ALONG THE EDGE OF THE TURQUOISE BAND FOR A PLAYFUL, FESTIVE LOOK.

DEFINE THE EYES WITH BLACK EYELINER, CREATING A SHARP WINGED EFFECT. FINISH WITH FALSE LASHES FOR A DRAMATIC FLAIR.

CHEEK DESIGN:

ADD A BRIGHT PINK BLUSH TO THE CHEEKS, BLENDING IT SOFTLY INTO THE SKIN. EXTEND THE BLUSH SLIGHTLY INTO THE TURQUOISE BAND FOR A SEAMLESS TRANSITION.

ADD MORE COLORFUL DOTS IN SHADES OF BLUE, PURPLE, AND GREEN ALONG THE OUTER EDGE OF THE BLUSH TO COMPLEMENT THE EYE DESIGN.

EYEBROWS:

SHAPE AND DEFINE THE EYEBROWS USING A DARK EYEBROW PENCIL OR FACE PAINT, ENSURING THEY ARE BOLD AND ARCHED TO MATCH THE INTENSITY OF THE EYE MAKEUP.

LIPS:

APPLY A BOLD PURPLE LIPSTICK USING A LIP BRUSH, ENSURING THE COLOR IS VIBRANT AND MATCHES THE PURPLE IN THE EYE MAKEUP.

FINAL TOUCHES:

ENSURE ALL COLORS ARE WELL-BLENDED AND THE DESIGNS ARE SYMMETRICAL. USE A SETTING SPRAY TO SECURE THE MAKEUP FOR LONG-LASTING WEAR.

COMPLETE THE LOOK WITH VIBRANT ACCESSORIES, SUCH AS A COLORFUL HAT OR EARRINGS, TO ENHANCE THE PLAYFUL AND WHIMSICAL THEME.

Carnival Chic

Base Color:

Apply a light foundation to create a smooth and even base over the entire face.

Eye Makeup:

Use a flat brush to apply vibrant purple eyeshadow across the eyelids, blending it outwards into a sharp, winged shape.

Add a pop of turquoise eyeshadow on the inner corners of the eyes, blending it into the purple for a seamless transition.

Use black eyeliner to create a bold winged line, extending it dramatically outwards. Apply false lashes for extra emphasis.

Add black dots under the eyes, starting from the inner corner and extending outward to enhance the playful look.

Cheek Design:

Apply a bright pink blush on the cheeks, blending it well into the skin for a soft, rosy look.

Add more black dots along the edge of the blush, creating a whimsical, dotted pattern that complements the eye makeup.

Eyebrows:

Shape and define the eyebrows using a dark eyebrow pencil or face paint, making them bold and arched to match the intensity of the eye makeup.

Lips:

Apply a bold pink lipstick using a lip brush, ensuring the color is vibrant and matches the pink in the blush.

Final Touches:

Ensure all designs are sharp and symmetrical. Use setting spray to secure the makeup for long-lasting wear.

Complement the look with colorful accessories, such as a top hat or bowtie, to enhance the fun, circus-like theme.

POP ART DOLL

BASE COLOR:

APPLY A LIGHT FOUNDATION TO CREATE A SMOOTH, EVEN BASE ON THE FACE.

EYE MAKEUP:

USE A FLAT BRUSH TO APPLY BRIGHT BLUE EYESHADOW AROUND THE EYES, EXTENDING IT OUTWARD IN A WINGED SHAPE.

ADD PINK EYELINER TO THE LOWER LASH LINE, AND USE A FINE BRUSH TO CREATE BLACK DOTS AND LASHES BELOW THE EYES FOR A DOLL-LIKE EFFECT.

FINISH THE EYES WITH BRIGHT PINK CONTACTS AND FALSE EYELASHES.

CHEEK CIRCLES:

WITH A ROUND BRUSH, PAINT BRIGHT PINK CIRCLES ON THE CHEEKS. MAKE SURE THE CIRCLES ARE PERFECTLY ROUND AND SYMMETRICAL.

FOREHEAD DETAIL:

USE A FLAT BRUSH TO PAINT A BLUE CIRCLE ON THE CENTER OF THE FOREHEAD, MATCHING THE EYESHADOW.

LIPS:

APPLY BRIGHT PINK LIPSTICK WITH A LIP BRUSH, CREATING A BOLD AND CLEAN FINISH.

FINAL TOUCHES:

ADD ANY FINAL DETAILS TO ENSURE SYMMETRY AND TOUCH UP WHERE NEEDED. USE SETTING SPRAY TO KEEP THE MAKEUP IN PLACE.

DARK ELEGANCE

BASE COLOR:

START WITH A NATURAL SKIN TONE, APPLYING A LIGHT FOUNDATION TO CREATE A SMOOTH, EVEN BASE ACROSS THE FACE.

EYE DESIGN:

USE A FLAT BRUSH TO APPLY BLACK FACE PAINT AROUND THE EYES, EXTENDING INTO SHARP, ANGULAR WINGS.

BLEND RED EYESHADOW WITHIN THE BLACK DESIGN, FOCUSING ON CREATING A GRADIENT EFFECT NEAR THE INNER CORNERS OF THE EYES.

EYEBROWS:

SHAPE AND DARKEN THE EYEBROWS WITH BLACK FACE PAINT OR AN EYEBROW PENCIL, GIVING THEM A SHARP, DEFINED ARCH.

LOWER EYE DETAIL:

EXTEND THE BLACK FACE PAINT BELOW THE EYES, CREATING A BOLD, TRIANGULAR SHAPE THAT TAPERS TOWARDS THE CHEEKS.

LIPS:

APPLY A BOLD RED LIPSTICK WITH A LIP BRUSH, MAKING SURE THE APPLICATION IS CLEAN AND PRECISE TO MATCH THE DRAMATIC EYE DESIGN.

FINAL TOUCHES:

ENSURE ALL ELEMENTS ARE SYMMETRICAL AND THE LINES ARE CRISP. USE SETTING SPRAY TO LOCK THE MAKEUP IN PLACE.

Dragon Empress

Base Color:

Apply a vibrant turquoise face paint evenly over the entire face and neck using a makeup sponge, creating a smooth, even base.

Scales and Horns Design:

Use a fine brush to paint blue and green scales on the forehead, extending down the bridge of the nose. Add darker blue or black shading around the edges of the scales to create depth.

Highlight the center of each scale with a lighter blue or white for a more realistic effect.

If you have costume horns, attach them at this point. Paint them with gold face paint, blending them into the forehead design seamlessly.

Eye Makeup:

Apply a deep blue eyeshadow around the eyes, blending it outward to mimic the shape of dragon eyes.

Use black eyeliner to create a sharp winged effect, extending it towards the temples. Finish with false lashes to enhance the dramatic, otherworldly look.

Golden Accents:

Paint golden vines or filigree patterns extending from the corners of the eyes towards the temples, enhancing the mystical dragon appearance.

Add a golden accent in the center of the forehead, above the scales, to act as a focal point.

Lips:

Apply red lipstick using a lip brush, ensuring the color is bold and striking. Add a touch of gold to the center of the lips for a metallic effect.

Final Touches:

Ensure all designs are sharp and symmetrical. Use a setting spray to lock in the makeup for long-lasting wear.

Complement the look with dragon-inspired accessories, such as scales on the neck or shoulders, to complete the transformation.

CARNIVAL DEMON

BASE COLOR:

APPLY WHITE FACE PAINT EVENLY OVER THE ENTIRE FACE USING A MAKEUP SPONGE TO CREATE A SMOOTH, EVEN BASE.

EYE MAKEUP:

USE A FLAT BRUSH TO APPLY BLUE EYESHADOW IN A TRIANGULAR SHAPE ABOVE AND BELOW THE EYES, EXTENDING THE TRIANGLES OUTWARD TOWARDS THE TEMPLES AND CHEEKS.

USE BLACK FACE PAINT TO OUTLINE THE BLUE TRIANGLES, ADDING SHARP, JAGGED LINES AT THE EDGES FOR A MORE DRAMATIC EFFECT.

DEFINE THE EYES WITH BLACK EYELINER, CREATING A BOLD WING THAT EXTENDS OUTWARD. FINISH WITH FALSE LASHES FOR ADDED INTENSITY.

FOREHEAD AND CHEEK DETAILS:

PAINT A SMALL RED DIAMOND SHAPE IN THE CENTER OF THE FOREHEAD USING A FINE BRUSH.

CREATE MATCHING RED AND BLACK DESIGNS ON THE CHEEKS, CURVING THEM UPWARD FROM THE CORNERS OF THE MOUTH TO EMPHASIZE THE SMILE. ADD SHARP POINTS TO GIVE THE DESIGN A SINISTER EDGE.

NOSE AND LIPS:

PAINT A SMALL BLACK OR RED TRIANGLE ON THE TIP OF THE NOSE, MIMICKING A CLASSIC CLOWN LOOK.

APPLY RED LIPSTICK TO THE LIPS, EXTENDING THE CORNERS SLIGHTLY WITH A FINE BRUSH TO MATCH THE CHEEK DESIGNS. ADD A SMALL RED DIAMOND SHAPE BELOW THE LOWER LIP FOR AN EXTRA DETAIL.

EYEBROWS:

SHAPE AND DARKEN THE EYEBROWS USING BLACK FACE PAINT OR AN EYEBROW PENCIL, CREATING A SHARP, ARCHED LOOK THAT COMPLEMENTS THE INTENSE EYE MAKEUP.

FINAL TOUCHES:

ENSURE ALL DESIGNS ARE SHARP, SYMMETRICAL, AND THE LINES ARE CLEAN. USE A SETTING SPRAY TO SECURE THE MAKEUP FOR LONG-LASTING WEAR.

COMPLETE THE LOOK WITH COSTUME ACCESSORIES LIKE HORNS OR A RUFFLED COLLAR TO ENHANCE THE PLAYFUL YET EERIE THEME.

Sinister Surgeon

Base Color:

Apply a light foundation evenly over the entire face to create a smooth, flawless base.

Eye Makeup:

Use a flat brush to apply red eyeshadow around the eyes, blending it outward toward the temples for a dramatic effect.

Define the eyes with black eyeliner, creating a sharp, winged line. Finish with false lashes for extra emphasis.

Add small red dots beneath the eyes to enhance the dramatic look.

Blood Effect on Forehead and Cheek:

Use a fine brush to paint a dripping blood effect starting from the forehead, with red paint dripping down toward the brow.

On one cheek, paint a larger splatter of red, allowing it to drip down in a natural way. Add a small black heart or symbol within the splatter for added detail.

Eyebrows:

Shape and define the eyebrows using a black eyebrow pencil or face paint, creating a sharp, arched look that complements the intense eye makeup.

Lips:

Apply a bold red lipstick using a lip brush, ensuring the color is vibrant and matches the red in the eye makeup and blood effects.

Final Touches:

Ensure all designs are sharp and the blood effects look realistic. Use setting spray to secure the makeup for long-lasting wear.

Complete the look with accessories, such as a lab coat or medical attire, to enhance the eerie, clinical theme.

BLOODSHOT SURGEON

BASE COLOR:

START BY APPLYING A LIGHT FOUNDATION EVENLY ACROSS THE ENTIRE FACE TO CREATE A SMOOTH, FLAWLESS BASE.

EYE MAKEUP:

APPLY VIBRANT RED EYESHADOW AROUND THE EYES, BLENDING IT OUTWARDS TOWARD THE TEMPLES FOR A DRAMATIC EFFECT.

USE BLACK EYELINER TO DEFINE THE EYES, CREATING A SHARP, WINGED LINE. ADD FALSE LASHES FOR EXTRA INTENSITY.

EXTEND THE RED EYESHADOW DOWNWARD, BLENDING IT INTO THE BLOOD EFFECTS ON THE FACE FOR A SEAMLESS LOOK.

BLOOD EFFECT ON FOREHEAD AND FACE:

WITH A FLAT BRUSH, PAINT A LARGE, DRIPPING BLOOD EFFECT STARTING FROM THE FOREHEAD AND EXTENDING DOWNWARDS ACROSS THE EYES AND NOSE. USE A DEEP RED FACE PAINT FOR THE MAIN SHAPE AND ADD DARKER TONES NEAR THE EDGES FOR DEPTH.

ENSURE THE BLOOD EFFECT IS SYMMETRICAL AND HAS NATURAL-LOOKING DRIPS THAT EXTEND TOWARD THE CHEEKS.

EYEBROWS:

SHAPE AND DARKEN THE EYEBROWS USING A BLACK EYEBROW PENCIL OR FACE PAINT, CREATING A BOLD, ARCHED LOOK THAT COMPLEMENTS THE INTENSE EYE MAKEUP.

LIPS:

APPLY A MATCHING RED LIPSTICK WITH A LIP BRUSH, ENSURING THE COLOR IS RICH AND COMPLEMENTS THE BLOOD EFFECTS ON THE FACE.

FINAL TOUCHES:

ENSURE ALL DESIGNS ARE SHARP, AND THE BLOOD EFFECTS LOOK REALISTIC AND THREE-DIMENSIONAL. USE A SETTING SPRAY TO KEEP THE MAKEUP IN PLACE THROUGHOUT YOUR EVENT.

COMPLETE THE LOOK WITH A WHITE LAB COAT OR SIMILAR ATTIRE TO ENHANCE THE EERIE, CLINICAL THEME.

FIERY FELINE

BASE COLOR:

APPLY A BLUE FACE PAINT EVENLY ACROSS THE ENTIRE FACE USING A MAKEUP SPONGE.

EYE MAKEUP:

USE A FLAT BRUSH TO PAINT A BOLD RED EYESHADOW AROUND THE EYES, EXTENDING IT OUTWARDS TOWARD THE TEMPLES.

WITH A FINE BRUSH, ADD BLACK EYELINER TO DEFINE THE EYES, CREATING A SHARP, WINGED LOOK. ADD FALSE LASHES TO ENHANCE THE EYES.

YELLOW FLAMES:

WITH A DETAIL BRUSH, PAINT YELLOW FLAME-LIKE PATTERNS ON THE CHEEKS, EXTENDING FROM THE EYES OUTWARD. ENSURE THE FLAMES ARE SHARP AND SYMMETRICAL.

LIPS:

APPLY A RICH RED LIPSTICK WITH A LIP BRUSH, ENSURING CLEAN, PRECISE EDGES.

FOREHEAD AND EARS:

IF YOU HAVE COSTUME EARS, APPLY THEM AT THIS STAGE. YOU CAN ALSO USE THE BLUE FACE PAINT TO BLEND THEM SEAMLESSLY WITH THE FACE.

ADD ANY FINAL DETAILS LIKE SHADING AROUND THE FOREHEAD TO CREATE DEPTH.

FINAL TOUCHES:

ENSURE ALL DESIGNS ARE SYMMETRICAL AND VIBRANT. USE A SETTING SPRAY TO KEEP THE MAKEUP INTACT.

Inferno Cat

Base Color:

Start with your natural skin tone as the base; no additional color needed.

Eye Makeup:

Apply bright yellow and orange eyeshadow around the eyes with a flat brush, blending outward into a sharp wing.

Use red eyeshadow to add depth around the lower eyelids, creating a dramatic gradient effect.

Define the eyes with black eyeliner, creating a sharp, winged look, and finish with false lashes.

Black and Yellow Flame Design:

With a detail brush, paint bold black and yellow flame-like patterns extending from the eyes onto the cheeks and temples. Ensure the flames are sharp and symmetrical.

Lips:

Apply black lipstick using a lip brush, making sure the edges are crisp and clean.

Forehead and Ears:

If using costume ears, apply them now. You can lightly shade them with black paint to blend with the overall look.

Add subtle black accents above the eyebrows to enhance the fierce look.

Final Touches:

Ensure all elements are balanced and vibrant. Use setting spray to keep the makeup in place throughout your event.

SHADOW FLAME FELINE

BASE COLOR:

APPLY A LIGHT GRAY FACE PAINT EVENLY OVER THE ENTIRE FACE USING A MAKEUP SPONGE.

EYE MAKEUP:

USE A FLAT BRUSH TO APPLY BOLD ORANGE AND YELLOW EYESHADOW AROUND THE EYES, BLENDING OUTWARD TOWARD THE TEMPLES.

ADD BLACK EYELINER WITH A FINE BRUSH TO DEFINE THE EYES, CREATING A SHARP, DRAMATIC WINGED EFFECT. FINISH WITH FALSE LASHES FOR ADDED INTENSITY.

BLACK FLAME PATTERNS:

USING A DETAIL BRUSH, PAINT BLACK FLAME-LIKE PATTERNS EXTENDING FROM THE EYES ACROSS THE TEMPLES AND CHEEKS. ENSURE THE FLAMES ARE SHARP AND SYMMETRICAL.

LIPS:

APPLY A BOLD RED LIPSTICK WITH A LIP BRUSH, MAKING SURE THE EDGES ARE CLEAN AND DEFINED.

FOREHEAD AND EARS:

IF USING COSTUME EARS, ATTACH THEM AT THIS POINT AND BLEND THEM WITH THE GRAY FACE PAINT.

ADD BLACK DETAILS ABOVE THE EYEBROWS TO ENHANCE THE DRAMATIC LOOK.

FINAL TOUCHES:

DOUBLE-CHECK THAT ALL DESIGNS ARE SYMMETRICAL AND VIBRANT. USE SETTING SPRAY TO KEEP THE MAKEUP IN PLACE THROUGHOUT THE DAY OR NIGHT.

Celestial Angel

Base Color:

Apply white face paint evenly over the entire face using a makeup sponge to create a smooth, angelic base.

Eye Design:

Use a flat brush to apply blue eyeshadow around the eyes, blending outward into a winged shape.

With a fine brush, outline the eyes with black face paint, creating sharp, feathered lines that extend upwards from the outer corners.

Forehead and Cheek Details:

Extend the black lines from the eye design upward onto the forehead, forming sharp, symmetrical patterns.

Add small black details in the center of the forehead and along the cheekbones to enhance the dramatic effect.

Eyebrows:

Darken and shape the eyebrows using black face paint or an eyebrow pencil, creating a bold and defined look.

Lips:

Apply deep red lipstick with a lip brush, ensuring clean and sharp edges to contrast with the white base.

Final Touches:

Ensure all designs are symmetrical and the lines are crisp. Use setting spray to lock the makeup in place. Optionally, add winged accessories to complete the angelic theme.

Frost Queen

Base Color:

Apply a light, pale foundation over the entire face to create a smooth, even base, emphasizing a ghostly, ethereal look.

Eye Design:

Use a flat brush to apply bright blue eyeshadow around the eyes, extending outward in a winged shape.

Add black eyeliner to define the eyes, creating a sharp, dramatic wing that extends toward the temples.

Lower Eye Detail:

With a fine brush, create black teardrop shapes extending from the lower eyelid to the top of the cheek, giving a dramatic, dripping effect.

Eyebrows:

Darken and sharpen the eyebrows using black face paint or a dark eyebrow pencil, giving them a strong, defined arch.

Lips:

Apply black lipstick with a lip brush, ensuring a clean and bold finish to contrast with the pale base color.

Final Touches:

Ensure all lines and designs are crisp and symmetrical. Use setting spray to keep the makeup in place throughout the event.

Noir Futurist

Base Color:

Start by applying a light foundation evenly across the face to create a smooth, flawless base.

Eye Design:

Use black face paint to create a bold, circular design around the eyes, extending outwards in a sharp, curved shape that wraps around the sides of the face. Ensure the design is symmetrical and smooth.

Apply black eyeshadow on the eyelids, blending it seamlessly into the circular design. Add a bit of silver or gray eyeshadow in the center of the eyelids for a touch of dimension.

Use black eyeliner to define the eyes, and apply false lashes to enhance the dramatic look.

Eyebrows:

Shape and define the eyebrows using a black eyebrow pencil or face paint, creating a sharp, arched look that complements the intense eye design.

Lips:

Apply black lipstick using a lip brush, ensuring the edges are crisp and the color is bold.

Cheek Detail:

Extend the black face paint from the eye design downwards in a sleek, curved line that accentuates the contours of the face.

Final Touches:

Ensure all designs are sharp, symmetrical, and the lines are clean. Use a setting spray to secure the makeup for long-lasting wear.

Complement the look with black, sleek accessories or clothing to enhance the futuristic, edgy theme.

GOTHIC GLAMOUR

BASE COLOR:

APPLY A LIGHT FOUNDATION TO CREATE A SMOOTH AND FLAWLESS BASE ON THE FACE, MAINTAINING A NATURAL SKIN TONE.

EYE DESIGN:

USE BLACK FACE PAINT TO CREATE A BOLD, SPIKY DESIGN EXTENDING FROM THE EYES OUTWARD. ENSURE THE SPIKES ARE SHARP AND SYMMETRICAL.

APPLY BLACK EYESHADOW ON THE EYELIDS, BLENDING IT INTO THE SPIKY DESIGN. ADD WHITE EYELINER OR EYESHADOW ALONG THE LOWER LASH LINE FOR CONTRAST.

EYEBROWS:

SHAPE AND DARKEN THE EYEBROWS USING BLACK FACE PAINT OR AN EYEBROW PENCIL, CREATING A DEFINED AND SHARP ARCH.

LIPS:

APPLY BLACK LIPSTICK WITH A LIP BRUSH, ENSURING A CLEAN AND BOLD FINISH THAT COMPLEMENTS THE DRAMATIC EYE DESIGN.

FOREHEAD AND CHEEK DETAILS:

USE A FINE BRUSH TO PAINT A SLEEK, CURVED BLACK LINE EXTENDING FROM THE FOREHEAD TOWARD ONE EYE FOR AN ELEGANT TOUCH.

LIGHTLY CONTOUR THE CHEEKS WITH A SOFT GRAY OR SILVER SHADE TO ADD DEPTH TO THE LOOK.

FINAL TOUCHES:

ENSURE ALL LINES AND DESIGNS ARE CRISP AND SYMMETRICAL. USE SETTING SPRAY TO SECURE THE MAKEUP FOR LONG-LASTING WEAR.

PHANTOM ELEGANCE

BASE COLOR:

APPLY A PALE, ALMOST WHITE FOUNDATION EVENLY OVER THE ENTIRE FACE TO CREATE A SMOOTH AND ETHEREAL BASE.

EYE DESIGN:

USE BLACK FACE PAINT TO CREATE A BOLD, SPIKY DESIGN AROUND THE EYES, EXTENDING OUTWARD IN A SYMMETRICAL PATTERN.

APPLY BLACK EYESHADOW ON THE EYELIDS, BLENDING IT SEAMLESSLY INTO THE SPIKY DESIGN FOR A DRAMATIC, GOTHIC LOOK. ADD WHITE EYELINER ALONG THE LOWER LASH LINE FOR CONTRAST.

EYEBROWS:

DARKEN AND SHAPE THE EYEBROWS USING BLACK FACE PAINT OR AN EYEBROW PENCIL, CREATING A DEFINED AND SHARP ARCH THAT COMPLEMENTS THE INTENSE EYE MAKEUP.

LIPS:

APPLY BLACK LIPSTICK USING A LIP BRUSH, ENSURING A CLEAN AND BOLD FINISH THAT MATCHES THE OVERALL MONOCHROMATIC THEME.

CHEEK CONTOURING:

LIGHTLY CONTOUR THE CHEEKS WITH A SOFT GRAY SHADE TO ADD DEPTH AND DIMENSION TO THE FACE, ENHANCING THE STRIKING BLACK AND WHITE CONTRAST.

FINAL TOUCHES:

ENSURE ALL DESIGNS ARE CRISP, WITH SHARP, CLEAN LINES. USE A SETTING SPRAY TO SECURE THE MAKEUP AND MAINTAIN ITS INTENSITY THROUGHOUT THE EVENT.

FLORAL SKULL BEAUTY

BASE COLOR:

APPLY AN EVEN LAYER OF WHITE FACE PAINT OVER THE ENTIRE FACE USING A MAKEUP SPONGE.

EYE DESIGN:

USE A FLAT BRUSH TO PAINT LARGE CIRCLES AROUND THE EYES WITH RED, ORANGE, AND YELLOW COLORS. BLEND FOR A GRADIENT EFFECT.

OUTLINE THE CIRCLES WITH BLACK PAINT, ADDING SCALLOPED EDGES WITH A FINE BRUSH.

NOSE AND MOUTH:

PAINT A BLACK TEARDROP SHAPE ON THE NOSE TIP USING A DETAIL BRUSH.

CREATE A STITCHED MOUTH EFFECT BY DRAWING BLACK LINES FROM THE LIPS ACROSS THE CHEEKS, WITH SMALL VERTICAL LINES INTERSECTING THEM.

FOREHEAD AND CHEEK DETAILS:

WITH A FINE BRUSH, PAINT BLACK SWIRLS, SPIDERWEBS, AND HEART SHAPES ON THE FOREHEAD AND CHEEKS. ADD COLORFUL DIAMONDS AND HEARTS FOR ACCENTS.

CHIN AND NECK DESIGN:

EXTEND THE DECORATIVE ELEMENTS TO THE CHIN AND NECK, MAINTAINING SYMMETRY WITH THE FACE USING BLACK AND COLORFUL PAINTS.

FLORAL ACCENTS:

ADD COLORFUL PAINTED FLOWERS OR ADHESIVE FACE JEWELS AROUND THE HAIRLINE AND CHEEKS TO ENHANCE THE FLORAL THEME.